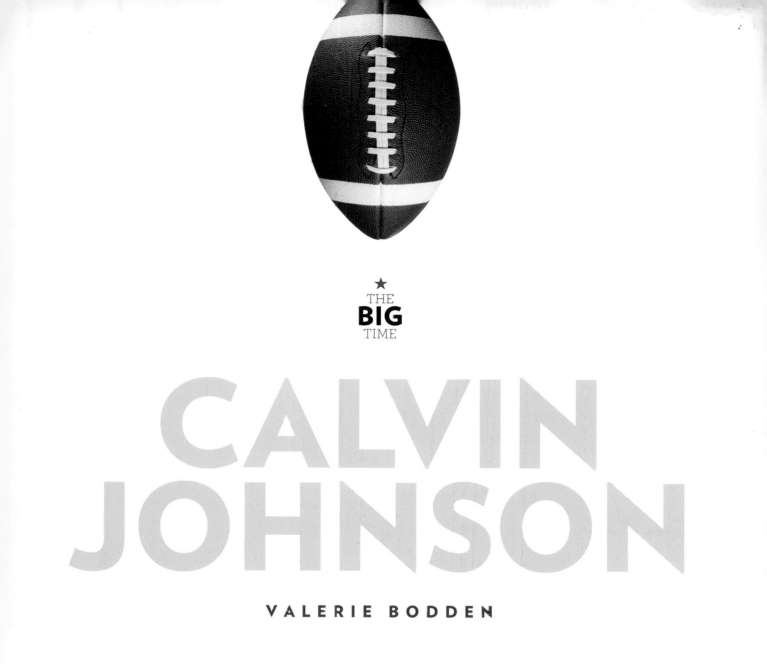

★
THE
BIG
TIME

CALVIN JOHNSON

VALERIE BODDEN

CREATIVE EDUCATION   CREATIVE PAPERBACKS

CALVIN JOHNSON

TABLE OF CONTENTS

Meet Calvin	**5**
Calvin's Childhood	**9**
Getting into Football	**11**
The Big Time	**15**
Off the Field	**19**
What Is Next?	**21**
What Calvin Says About ...	**23**

Glossary	Read More	Websites	Index
24	**24**	**24**	**24**

MEET CALVIN

Calvin races down the football field. Suddenly, he turns and grabs the football that is flying toward him. He pushes past defenders and runs for the **end zone**. Touchdown!

Calvin Johnson is a wide receiver for the Detroit Lions. He runs fast, jumps high, and makes amazing catches. Fans call him "Megatron" because he is big and powerful like the Transformers robot.

Every year, Calvin and the Detroit Lions play a game on Thanksgiving.

CALVIN'S CHILDHOOD

Calvin was born September 29, 1985, and grew up in Tyrone, Georgia. He lived with his parents, two sisters, and a brother. Calvin's parents would not let their kids play sports unless they got good grades.

Calvin's dad likes to watch him play football.

TYRONE, GEORGIA

GETTING INTO FOOTBALL

Calvin started playing baseball when he was five. But his mom would not let him play football until he was 12. She was afraid he would get hurt.

....

In 2012, Calvin got to throw out the first pitch at a Detroit Tigers baseball game.

In high school, Calvin was one of the best wide receivers in the country. In 2004, Calvin started college at Georgia Tech. He studied business *management* and played football. In 2006, he won the Biletnikoff Award as the best wide receiver in college football.

. . . .

Calvin made 178 receptions for the Georgia Tech Yellow Jackets.

THE BIG TIME

In 2007, Calvin decided to skip his last year of college to play in the National Football League (NFL). The Detroit Lions **drafted** him. He was the second player picked in the NFL Draft that year.

....

Calvin celebrates with his Lions team-mates after they win a game (left).

In Calvin's first season, he caught 48 passes for 756 yards. He made five touchdowns. In 2010, Calvin was chosen for the **Pro Bowl** for the first time. In 2012, he had 1,964 receiving yards. That broke an NFL record!

....

Calvin is 6-foot-5 and weighs 236 pounds.

OFF THE FIELD

When Calvin is not playing football, he spends time in Georgia. In 2008, he set up the Calvin Johnson Jr. Foundation. The group gives football camps, feeds needy families, and helps student athletes pay for school.

....

Calvin has fun teaching young athletes how to stay strong and healthy.

WHAT IS NEXT?

In Calvin's first six years in the NFL, the Lions had only one winning season. But Calvin wanted to help make the team better. In 2012, he signed an eight-year deal with the Lions. He hoped to someday lead his team to the Super Bowl!

....

In the 2013 season, Calvin and the Lions placed third in their division.

WHAT CALVIN SAYS ABOUT ...

ENTERING THE NFL

"It's been the one place I've wanted to be since I started playing football."

LOSING

"You can't get down and think things won't get better, or they definitely won't."

PLAYING THROUGH INJURIES

"I'm not going to be the kind of guy who's going to say 'I can't do this or this because I'm hurt.'"

GLOSSARY

drafted picked to be on a team; in a sports draft, teams take turns choosing players

end zone the end of the football field, where a team must get the ball for a touchdown

management the act of controlling or directing the way a business or organization is run

Pro Bowl a football game in which the best players in the NFL play against one another

READ MORE

Ellenport, Craig. *Wideouts*. New York: Scholastic, 2012.

Gigliotti, James. *National Football League Game Breakers*. New York: Scholastic, 2009.

Savage, Jeff. *Calvin Johnson*. Minneapolis: Lerner, 2013.

WEBSITES

Lions Youth Programs
http://www.detroitlions.com/youth-programs/
This is the kids' site of Calvin's team, the Detroit Lions.

The Official Site of Calvin Johnson
http://bigplaycj.com/main/
Calvin Johnson's official page is filled with information, pictures, and videos.

INDEX

Biletnikoff Award 12
Calvin Johnson Jr. Foundation 19
childhood 9, 11, 12
college 12, 15
Detroit Lions 7, 15, 21
family 9, 11
Georgia Tech 12
high school 12
interests 19
NFL Draft 15
nickname 7
Pro Bowl 16
receiving yards 16
Tyrone, Georgia 9

PUBLISHED BY Creative Education and Creative Paperbacks
P.O. Box 227, Mankato, Minnesota 56002
Creative Education and Creative Paperbacks
are imprints of The Creative Company
www.thecreativecompany.us

DESIGN AND PRODUCTION BY Christine Vanderbeek
PRINTED IN the United States of America

PHOTOGRAPHS BY Alamy (epa european pressphoto agency b.v., ZUMA Press, Inc.), Corbis (David Bergman, REBECCA COOK/Reuters, Greg Drzazgowski/Icon SMI, David Duprey/AP, RALPH D. FRESO/Reuters, MSA/Icon SMI, Paul Sakuma/AP), Getty Images (Diamond Images, Gregory Shamus), iStockphoto (AnthiaCumming, Pingebat), Newscom (Gary C. Caskey/UP)

LIBRARY OF CONGRESS CATALOGING-IN-PUBLICATION DATA
Bodden, Valerie.
Calvin Johnson / Valerie Bodden.
p. cm. — (The big time)
Includes index.
Summary: An elementary introduction to the life, work, and popularity of Calvin Johnson, a professional football star wide receiver for the Detroit Lions who is known as "Megatron."

ISBN 978-1-60818-494-1 (HARDCOVER)
ISBN 978-1-62832-076-3 (PBK)
1. Johnson, Calvin, 1985– —Juvenile literature. 2. Football players—United States—Biography—Juvenile literature. I. Title.
GV939.J6123B64 2014
796.332092—dc23 [B]   2014000248

CCSS: RI.1.1, 2, 3, 4, 5, 6, 7; RI.2.1, 2, 5, 6, 7; RI.3.1, 5, 7, 8; RI.4.3, 5; RF.1.1, 3, 4; RF.2.3, 4

FIRST EDITION
9 8 7 6 5 4 3 2 1

Note: Every effort has been made to ensure that the websites listed above are suitable for children, that they have educational value, and that they contain no inappropriate material. However, because of the nature of the Internet, it is impossible to guarantee that these sites will remain active indefinitely or that their contents will not be altered.